Solstice *SUMMER*

A QUARTERLY OF ARTS

PUBLISHED INDEPENDENTLY

C000045509

Editor-in-Chief
Kaylyn Dunn

Editorial Staff
Darius Muller
Madison Pollum
Tatiana Woodly

Sponsored by
Kada's Bookstore

https://www.solsticeliterarymagazine.com/

To submit, go to:
https://www.solsticeliterarymagazine.com/submissions

Cover Art by Kaylyn Dunn

Contents

Introduction

IDENTITY. EVERYONE has one. *Everyone.*

Some are printed out on legal documents.

Some are told to friends as introductions.

Some are a series of scribbled notes used to remember ourselves.

But everyone has an identity. A way to describe one's own personhood. A way to explain how they see themselves. Over time each person needs to way to make themselves recognizable among the crowd.

In this issue, 15 writers have gotten on that theme. The following stories and poems explore the different aspects of identity. Not only that of themselves, but of the world around them.

My Grandpa

Pauline Aksay

On the day my Grandpa died
My mother gripped the phone so tight
Tears were flowing from her eyes
The first time I had seen her cry

On the day my Grandpa died
A hurricane wrecked my insides
He'd always said that he'd been fine
Limping to place the trash outside

On the day my Grandpa died
Hope had shattered as I realized
All the screams and heated fights
He'd tried to keep the peace and quiet

On the day my Grandpa died
I remembered every time
All the stories about his life
All the horrors he'd survived...

His father and the Genocide
His feet that had turned to the side
Consistently being despised
By his mother all the time
Conscription and the brutal fights
Three days that he had spent blind
Asbestos that wasn't purified
Countless fear and sleepless nights

And all the pain he kept inside
All the times he'd sacrificed
Limping to place the trash outside

Never once did he not smile

Except the day my Grandpa died
When he fell from a stroke inside
And earned his wings to be beatified
The saint I'll miss till the end of time.

Here

Rammel Chan

To our great surprise, there aren't very many lifeforms that look like humans out in the Galaxy. Movies and TV shows had us thinking that every sentient alien would have a head on their shoulders, two legs, a spine, a brain and a little four chambered heart, but it turns out this form is rare in the cosmos.

Humans like to travel. We like to see. So, we fly through the slipstream, traveling at super luminous speeds in boxes of metal in the ether that connects the light matter. Despite being small and generally unremarkable, you can find a human being pretty much everywhere. We are an odd bustling diaspora.

Some sentient aliens are friendly. Some sentients are not. Some sentients see us as a kind of attraction, strange exotic little things with odd ways from far beyond. Some sentients yank us out of their bars for being too loud and under their alien skies beat us to death with g'rannixaball bats. Like we were animals.

Most though are nice. Put us to work. Give us food. Antimatter. We go through the cosmos in search for a friendly place, lots to do, air that's breathable, land that could be a home.

Every human we see now is a welcome face. The absurd notion that a dark-skinned human is somehow untrustworthy or a human with little eyes and olive skin is somehow suspicious becomes unimportant when your employer is an intelligent caterpillar the size of a house, with liquid lithium flowing through their veins.

Our self-hatred washed itself out against the ocean of the universe.

On the new worlds we find we are quartered off in our little human parts of town. Aliens with lizard skin and breath as hot as lava visit and walk through our streets where we've built replicas of human places from back on Earth. The Parthenon. The Eiffel Tower. The Great pyramids. They laugh at our stinky human food. Our hamburgers. Our spaghetti. Our burritos. Our dim sum. They pick up a crucifix and laugh and wonder what it means. They tickle Christ's armpits, and they toss it into their alien air like a toy.

After an alien century a human goes to an alien school. We sit in giant chairs not built for bipedal creatures. Our name will be something like Alice Washington or Martin Kien, but at any given moment, if we were ever asked, we have our alien name ready too. But no one asks.

And the other youngsters mock and laugh at us. Make fun of our two tiny hands. Our two tiny legs. Our strange smooth skin. Our tiny eyes. What are those bits of filthy string that sit on the top of their round head! They say these things at high volume, thinking that the little human child doesn't understand, not knowing that our ears are implanted with Universal Translators that gather alien words like water and floods a human heart to breaking.

And we go. We find and cling fast to our purposes. We build sturdy farms of alien fruits on a planet where once was thought nothing could grow. We tag along to a hardy crew of malcontent slugs whose only joy is mining asteroids for precious stones. We serve in a bar

9

where we sling poisonous concoctions to gargantuan amoebic travelers from across the Spiral. We learn and we teach. We embed ourselves in institutions of study, where minds from an infinity of worlds attempt to solve the problems of infinity. And every night, as bowties are undone and hands shake ommatophores and the alien moons rise to their zenith, we sit down and these new friends flick their tongues at us, "You're a fine little creature! Where is your homeworld? Where are you from?"

And we give them a smile they have yet to learn to understand, and we say, "Here."

And they laugh or come to their alien proximity to laughter. They pass us a flask of Ionioni whiskey. They slap our soft backs with rough paws the color of auroras. They think it's a joke, but it's true. Because this is what a human does best and what defines a human the best: our home is where we belong and wherever in the universe we belong, we can make our home.

Weddings between sentient aliens and humans are a fun affair. Joyous days when cultures amalgamate, become one out of many. We are dressed in blue suits, black tuxes, beautiful flowery hanboks, colorful lehengas and pure white gowns and they will stand ten feet tall, gangly clumsy tentacles evolved for navigating seas of mercury, tied in little silken bows. And they will share our beds, they whose skin is the noncolor of dark matter, whose touch is static and whose voices vibrates like the baritone hums of Mongols chanting. They will rest their inky appendages on our skin and bone, and they will learn a new way to love by loving us.

No wars are fought in this brave new world like we saw
on TV. It's just the infinite war of wanting to be seen
and being seen as nothing. Some sentients will love us,
yes, want to protect us and understand us. Yet still,
some sentient aliens will see our bodies as expendable,
disposable, easily plucked like turnips from the ground,
for their consumption, for their pleasure.

After another alien century, we will stand a foot taller.
The gravity, the food, the culture, changes our form.
We will dress in the alien fashion. We will stand in the
alien way. We will seek ways to change our bodies,
wearing false legs, false arms, and distorting our eyes
with surgery or color in order to look more "beautiful",
more like them. We will speak in new tongues with
accented human voices. We will not long for blue skies,
or the taste of mangoes, or the smell of smoky lapsang.
We will not yearn for the sounds of trickling water, of
starlings singing, of the mourning of a cello, or to see
the orange creamsicle vision of a single yellow sun
rising over Lake Michigan.

By then, we will truly be from "Here."

Oh, but how we find each other still. Across a sea of
green skin, a young girl in Hobardi dress sees another
girl with her head on her shoulders and two legs and
presumably a spine and a brain and a little four
chambered heart. What an odd-looking thing.

It begins with a wave, then a smile, warm and
surprising. Then two credits worth of Valvaxan tea
later.
Where are you from?

My mother's mother is from Port Andradi on Othos. It's a human colony on the Perseus Arm. I know Othos. It's nice.
Yeah.
I'm sorry, but where are you really from?
Like, originally originally?
Yeah.
Oh. Uh. I think Earth.
Me too! Do you know where exactly?
I couldn't say. I don't know much about Earth. Do you?
A little. My father's ancestors colonized Europa. He was a sailor during the refugee crisis that's how we ended up in Hobardiim.
Got it.

I don't mean to be rude.
It's not rude.
It is rude.
Not when you ask it.
I only ask, because I was trying to do some research at the Temple, and I discovered that I might be from…
Cincinnati.
Cincinnati? What system is that in?
It's a city on Earth.
Really! That's so cool. How do you know?
This book. Look at the girl in this picture.
She looks just like…
Doesn't she!
…
It might be stupid. There's so many Earthling places and different types of Earthlings who lived in so many different types of places. I could be from anywhere! But I was just drawn to her, you know? Her nose.
She could be your great-great grandmother!

Laughter.

How long are you going to be studying at the Temple?
I graduate in 2 years.
Wow. Me too.
…
I don't mean to talk shit, but I hate the Yrrg-zai acolytes.
Oh they're the worst.
Have you ever been talked down to by…
Oh yes.
That tone!
They talk like we don't understand.
I have a PhD in Xenolinguistics. I understand.

Laughter.

The other day a priestess grabbed me.
Really?
You know that section in the dining hall where the
Orderdines? I had spilled some food, so I decided to
walk through them to the bathroom and they just…
Did they think you were…?
I guess, they just saw THIS and made their assumptions.
I'm so sorry.
It's ok. It's fine. It's FINE.
Did you get hurt?
…a little.
Did you notify…
Yes. Nobody did anything. It's stupid. It's my fault
anyway.
…
…
No. It's not.
It's not?
Of course, it is not. What an Ygarl-malil.

Laughter.

I'm sorry.
No it's ok!
Do you want a tissue?
I dunno. For some reason…
It feels good to talk about it, yeah?
It's like we have our own…
Shorthand!
Yeah! I feel it too.
…
Of course, it's not ALL bad.
No! It's not.
But…
But…
…
To say this to you and for you to just hear it. To see your
face as I say it. It feels really good! …
It's really cool to have met you.
I know. I feel the same.
We should meet up again.
I don't have very many Earthling friends.
I have like zero Earthling friends.
Actually I have like negative Earthling friends.
I only have Earthling enemies.

Laughter.

What's your slip address.
Here's mine.
What do you want to do?
Tea's good!
I love tea!
There's a Human town in Ghibben City that I've been
meaning to check out. Let's do it. Maybe we can find
out more about Cincinnati! Oh! Yes. Please!
Great.

Great.

…

See you then.
See you then.

See you then.

Wishes

William E. Heston

*Previously published in the *Pennsylvania Bards Eastern PA Poetry Review 2021*

"What would you do if you had millions of dollars?"
The man asks the cashier at the corner store,
Who is ringing up his gallon of milk
And stauffer's lasagna dinners.
They talk about Bezos,
They talk about the forbes list,
And whoever is on those magazines
At the checkout stand.
"I'm still waitin' on the first million!"
The cashier replies.

A block away,
The sixty-something busboy wanders outside the diner,
Eyes pointed nowhere, his open-toothed smile
Being his default expression.
The cook, leaning behind the counter inside, scoffs:
"Yeah, he's a couple screws loose!"

The woman stands on the platform at noon, in
The heart of the city, with
The boy who is now a man
Wrapped in her arms,
Wearing a UCLA shirt, as
His duffle bag lay at his feet.
"I don't know if I'll ever see you again,"
She says sweetly.
In the distance,
The rumble of the train crescendos.

The girl plays her new acoustic
On a bench by the river adjacent to the station,
Watching the sun fall below the Philly skyline.
"I just wanted to see America,"
She explains to the stranger who stopped to listen.
"I see it so much in movies,
And always wanted to travel this country,
And I think I needed music
For that."

"I honestly don't know what to do,"
My friend Stacy tells me. We went to high school
together,
And now we're half a decade removed,
Sitting in her car at 8 pm on my break,
A year after she graduated college,
As her boyfriend waits with dinner at home. She says,
"You at least have that, an idea. Don't you?"

Midnight at the inner-city bus station:
A woman whose leathery-skin
Puts her at seventy years old,
Raspy voice telling of fifty years smoking experience,
And a matted fur coat and knotted hair,
Reminisces about her looks
In her youth,
As the man next to her pulls out an oranged-topped
needle.

I wait for the bus to pull up an hour from now,
On this chilly night,
Heading home to my parents' house
From my second-shift packing job,
Holding a book of scribbled-out poetry
Under my arm.

I want to tell my friend
That I do.

Murder of Crows

William E. Heston

Dedicated to all my friends in the rock & metal scene,
for you have made me feel at home.

I only heard the news in passing,
Slinking through the cold, white-lit aisles of the
Walmart Supercenter,
Domesticated by docility,
Filling the awkward silence with tuneless humming
When the murder of crows, in their studded jackets,
scattered about,
Cooed their news:
"On the pier, behind the store, 10 pm sharp."

Here's what you need to know
Before you enter the underground:
Wolves may burrow in the dirt,
But they only hunt on the surface.

So I marched with others
Of painted-canvas skin
And pierced lips,
Ill-fitted flannels
And eye-shadow,
Passing under puddles of industrial lamplight,
Feeling my heart come to match the tempo of
Of those machine gun blast beats in the distance.

Like sickness, the word spread.
Like sickness, I've been twisting
My thoughts, aching for a new set of bruised lungs
Whose breath gets lost in the echo of amplifiers
Raging chainsaw riffs into the midnight sky.

Like possession I follow the piping screams
Down the pitch-black asphalt path,
Fenced off behind the parking lot
At the waterfront.

We slip through the sheared wire-gate,
Gazing in wonder at the alien blacklights
Spilling through the urban overgrowth.
Phone lights erratically illuminate our footsteps,
No longer careful,
We rush toward the circle-pit at the edge of the pier.

Punk Rock John has never been more proud.

Twenty-five years
Of internalized violence
Exorcized in an unbroken scream,
Drowned by grimey bass
And cries for anarchy.

Despite it being damn near freezing,
Our bodies still sweat as we get tossed
Through the pit
Barely dodging the band, storming and swinging
Around the firecrackers igniting the sky from the
epicenter.

I am face to war-painted face
With the singer,
Howling out the words to songs I've never heard before,
Until my breath is fire,
Until my body folds like wet paper,
Until my voice has all the melody of a detuned guitar
And my feet are burning coals.

***

Well after midnight.
The bands have packed up.
The concrete pier is tracked with boot prints and pyro
shells,
And the remaining traces of cigarette smoke linger,

Ghostly, in the freshwater breeze.
The last bus has departed.
I hobble down the avenue,
With my friend Caleb's house key in hand,
And his number pulled up on my phone,
As a couch waits for me tonight.
The traffic stream is empty now,

And the last cars pull out of the lots of the strip clubs
That dot the neighborhood.
I finally feel safe in the silence,
Between my ringing ears,
Beside the purring river waves.

April's 1st New Moon Special

Sponge-Grass

Mehreen Ahmed

I stood on a patch of grass in the wetlands. I called it the sponge-grass. If one were to step on it, the sponge-grass patch, typically, sprung up and down under one's feet movement, not submerge completely. This porous patch of the drenched grass, as resilient as it was held up some promise of stability, but not a whole lot.

Standing on it, I also watched birds through handheld binoculars at a distance. Today, I watched something spectacular—the rare ospreys. I almost thought they had disappeared from this part of the globe—the wetlands. Almost, they never flew in here at all. But here they were, today, alive and well.

The ospreys helped my mood to turn around. I was in a downward trajectory of my writing career. My blues had reached its outer limits with all the rejections I'd received in one day. Doubts gnawed at me like termites. That perhaps I was deluding myself as a writer. Perhaps, I should leave writing with the more sophisticated minds, and be an astute reader in its stead—less stress and more enjoyment—win-win. This self-flagellation of despair was a trigger towards being a defeatist—a quitter, which I was not.

At a difficult moment like this, I had met him. A random guy whom I dared to choose online from my friend's list. That I was so bored, I wanted to do something—anything. It had all started with a song. I had recorded a song and sent it through to him via messenger. The response was almost immediate. He sent me back one of his voice-recorded song clips, but deaf to the tune. By far, I least sang in tune. I thought this exchange was funny listening to his off-tune songs which he sang so much in earnest to impress me, taking the trouble of recording and sending them through.

I took this in the spirit of a short-lived craze until the boredom was gone. A few exchanges of songs, what bad could come out of this? I took the liberty to trifle with him. At one point, I decided to end it. The sweetness was turning sour. I wrote to him THE END. Immediately, the phone rang. As I looked at the screen, his name came up. My heart skipped a beat. I did the most unusual thing. I took the call. I could feel some trepidation in his voice, too. It quivered.

He asked,"What did you mean, 'THE END?'"

"It meant what it means, END of this? That we don't sing to each other anymore. And no more contact."

"What? Why? Why did you even start it then? If I knew this was how it was going to end, I would not have sung at all. Your fault, you started this."

His words were ringing through like an incisive jab, as he blamed me squarely.

"What do you want?" I asked him. "A few friendly exchanges of off-tune notes, not even proper singing. That's all— and that's all there is to it. "

He said, "No, there has to be more to it. These were not empty songs. These were love songs, and they meant a lot to me. They interpreted into something more than just frivolous, as you put it. I want this relationship to deepen—I want to bind it further."

"You will not do any such thing?" I yelled.

"Just watch me," he said.

He hung up at that moment but sent through a bunch of poems which he had written over many years, complimenting on my looks, my eyes, my hands—and how beautiful I was. That he was already in a relationship with me.

Wait a minute? What relationship? Had he been stalking me all those years that he had been on my friend list? It appeared to me that given half a chance, he would start making love to me online. And the sexting had already ensued. This puzzled me a great deal, and I thought this surely was a scam. But he was relentless, and not backing out. He continued to send me a deluge of off-tune songs again, but beautiful love poems written in a half-formed second language meant for me as he didn't speak my language too well. I laughed at first and even tried to block him.

But the next day, I unblocked him thinking that he was probably right. It was all my fault—my stupid idea which led to this. I may have taken this as a game. But I should have thought this through before I embarked. I hadn't thought of its consequences. But who knew it would end up like this? If only I had even a quarter of a notion of how this would affect him, I would not have indulged in this at all. However, could I trust him, though?

Trust—whatever was happening was all in songs and fantasy alone, not anyone's lived experience. It was the fastest depleting value, anyway. This declaration of romance for me, could it be that he was faking it—all in the same spirit of jest? He texted me saying that he had been my online friend for seven years. But he never had the courage to speak to me. He had the maddest desire to live with me, make love to me, make me a part of him. He found me soft and sensitive and could not get over me—not today, not in a million years.

Those words astounded me. How extraordinary? I tried to remember what he looked like. So much for friendship; I hardly even noticed his posts. He was a cold number on my friend list as far as I was concerned. Nothing to rave about. And today, this? I started thinking about him. Suddenly, I began to take those poems, not his songs, more seriously. As I read through them one poem at a time, I felt I was being drawn into its musicality, its lyrics, as simultaneously as I was trying to block him.

They were beautiful. Even in those broken words. I realized that all of his poems were not about me, my looks, or his fascination for me. But about other girls too, who looked different to me. His passionate compliments of their fair looks, their blonde hair, and their perfumed bodies lit an ugly fire inside me—jealousy. There was s situation. It was getting out of hand, not the way I had intended to address my boredom by a long shot.

I began to feel an alien emotion—a mad rush, surging within me. This man online did not even speak my language, only broken. One, whom I had ignored for seven long years. Now that I had actually looked at his pictures, I found him quite charming. The more I looked, the more, I saw him—an innocence on his face—his captivating smiles.

Indeed. These rare desires seemed to have found a home in my heart. I tried to switch them off. I was mystified how his gentle persuasions were affecting me. I was gradually slipping into his grips of some kind of magical power. This, I thought was totally not me. I blocked him again. And again, I unblocked him straightaway, and repeatedly until I decided that I was going to stop doing this—I missed him—I was actually missing him? How was this possible? Regardless, I had to see him, his pictures every day, see the green button on top of my screen to know that he was logged in. That he was well and was writing poetry profusely. But I couldn't respond to his advances—the strange demands he made—the urgency of kissing him on his video calls; because making love online was not my feat, neither had I signed up for this.

What had begun as a childish prank to adjust my state of boredom transpired into this? When he insisted, coaxed in fact, trying to convince me with those romantic words which he executed so well, even half-formed to ignite arousal in me—romance which had never been my forte, but was a rare emotion. No—nope—this wasn't me. I had been beguiled. I argued and became determined to block him from my thoughts, at least. But his love poems kept coming through, slowly albeit regularly, overpowering me.

Those written words. "I have everything in my life except one thing, and that's you. Do you not hear the sounds of my beating heart at all, the unspoken words of my soul? You're my love. You're the only one, in my life. Kiss me. Kiss me, my love. No one likes me; they move away like waves. Am I not good-looking enough?"

I felt a stir within me. I would have to be spectacularly stone-hearted otherwise if those words didn't move me. Still, it was way too condescending for me to respond to this man whom I had hardly known to violate my rules to make love to him online. I couldn't trust him! That was it. My logic had finally kicked in!

In the heart of it, this unresolved and un-relinquished burning sprinted through my heart. The more I nursed it, the more pronounced it became. But there was no other way around. Why? I was charmed by the lyrics of his

poetry, even though they didn't mean much in my language, apart from its sweet sound, which had transformed meaningfully when translated into his own; I understood so well. Too well. Those poetic expressions sung in full tune; they were refined and profound, as I snared myself into those woven words. Until I had my back against the wall.

It made me forget that demise may be waiting in the offing. My emotions were raw and immature, his wasn't—those words proved it. As I processed them more and more discretely, they made sense down to the last phoneme, I could forget-him-not. Was it really my fault? That I had opened a world of lyrical fantasy through this? Looking back on it now, perhaps it was, but fanning love certainly was not in the plan, strictly with a man online. Who was linguistically challenged in mine but sweet-tongued, in which he pursued this uncomely romance?

I asked him if we could ever meet face to face? He was uncannily quiet for some time. I kept looking at the screen, thinking *where are you now*? Then came the bombshell.

"No, not really— never actually—I am married and I can't leave my wife because she is disabled. Love never dies. I love you…I love only you. I don't feel romance for anyone else."

How could I be so blind? Was I so wrapped up in these enchantments, like a sobby sponge that I allowed myself to plunge into this kind of non-reality? Distrust reared its ugly head. I thought, was there any exchange of love at all between us beyond the music and poetry across the two languages? Perhaps, it was all about the love of the words alone. Unlike his songs, his poetry was far too beautiful to ignore. Were those urgent love-filled video calls, pleading me to kiss him and to make love to him partly his poetic passions unlocking?

Which might had been fine by him, I thought the next afternoon, as I stood in the same place? It should have been fine by me too. We were after all two lonesome, stale-mated hearts interlocked within the framework of an infinite stream of tune, upended. Conflicting, even stifling sometimes, I stood on an unnerving patch of the sponge-grass on the edge of the great ospreys 'thriving breeding grounds, we stood our metaphorical ground.

Just in that moment, when I felt some relief as to how I was in love with his poems only, not really him, his message came through.

He wrote. "I cannot get you out of my head."

I read that and asked him if he had ever loved anyone else, online. There was a pause in his reply as I waited.

His short reply, "Yes."

My immediate response—"Did you make love to them too, online? How do you know so much about this stuff?"

He replied, "Yes" again. But I love you, I didn't love them. I only made out with them, online. They were really good— "advanced" not like you, at all. Why? You said—you said, you hated it, no?"

"Indeed, I did. And will continue to do so."

He wrote. "Still, I only want you, You're the only one for me. You give me the energy to take care of my wife. You are the reason why I can do what I do, my muse too."

I quickly logged out and continued to watch the birds of prey through the handheld binoculars. The sponge-grass under my feet felt like a dull door-mat.

I shook myself and woke up from a trance I was drowning in. I made a decision, whether or not to help him or move away. I tried to block him, many times. But I couldn't. Hence, I changed my tactics. I tried to focus on him instead of my emotions which were getting in the way. Clearly, I saw a desperate, young man in need of assurance; low self-esteem because of body image; living with an invalid wife who starved him of sex. I felt I was finally getting a fuller picture. No, I couldn't move away. I decided to support him. I told him that he was handsome, he was young, he had money, he had a cute smile and above all he was a poet.

"Do you know what's lacking, though?" he asked. "You—I don't have you in my life. Your love, only your love can make me complete."

"I love you, too. Only, I can't make love to you on cam. Can you understand that?"

"You don't love me at all," he said and logged off.

Seriously? How was I even going to make romance on the web, except in love songs? I felt naive and silly. His poems had already touched me. But I had to know that I could also keep my boundaries. How far was I going to go to help this man boost his confidence so he could get on with his life? There were all these questions jamming in my mind, in futility. I had to wait it out to find how far down the road this relationship was taking me, knowing that he had mated with many on the net. I texted my soul to him and he sexted it back. However, both were doing wonders for one another. That I found him attractive, I liked to see him grow. He was going to get his poetry book out on romantic poems. I flirted with the idea that I could be his dark lady.

Six months had passed. He debuted his book of poems. He acknowledged me and his invalid wife. He had already crossed the boundaries in our relationship, a long time; It was only me holding back. However, his success gave him access to others. It gave him a strange kind of high. Fans, young girls flocked around him, going crazy over his magical lyrics. He was beginning to distance himself from me. He called them gfs who were only too eager to make love to him online.

It was time to let him go. But I still couldn't. My internal logic kicked in, again. What about his wife? Between them, I had acted as a catalyst by changing the complexion of that relationship? No?" In a ground-breaking resolve to instill courage into him, my resolve was gradually thinning. While he continued to make love to those gfs online—they were just "satisfying flings," he said, while I was always in the center, because I was his only true love. Music to my ears, I lay low like a dove in a pigeon-hole—lightning throbbed a heart behind the distant translucent clouds; it sparked the stuff of life, not a fancy.

She is the Moon

Dani Kei Jochums

Can I **be** a whisper?
Could he hear me singing?
Could he hear me screaming?
Which **am** I doing now?
Can I be a shy
sky sly giggle
behind
delicate fan
hands? Blush
in my cheek
says spring
flower.
Color in my skin says winter snow.
And speaking of snow – we ran out.
Now I will run out of heat.
I will **be** airless.

Thunder **is** cackling.
Lightening **is** cracking.
Is crashing, **is** tackling
Does everything have to scream?
This house **is** swaying.
This house **is** spinning.
It **is** a ballroom dancer.
The orchestra **is** out of control. It might as well **be**
trombones erupting but instead it **is** thumping as he
beats at the floor.
He **is** angry.

She showed up before the sprinkle cascaded into storm. Behind her, the crescent moon broke through the night clouds. A smile broke out over his face, his laugh, a riot of sound looking out.

"Look who it **is**."

The
physical
body enters
through
the front
door, all
pale skin
and dark
eyes, jeans
and genes
and
patchwork
fuckup
everything.
But the
mind – she
doesn't
mind- **was**
left
somewhere
a long time
ago. These
days it
came for
visits
exclusively
at
inconvenient times,
midnight
instead of
noon tea.

His teeth ground the meat into a pulp. They **were** sitting across from each other at the battered oak table. Most times he did not look at her, but when he did, his sharp eyes poked and prodded at her. Her eyes **were** similarly pointed in their wanderings, looking at the definitions of his muscles, the scratchy shadow along his jaw.

He smiled into the silence, sharp shining smile that **is** his family inheritance, that smile so much like Luke's. She pretended not to feel the jump in her stomach. She couldn't feel if it **was** lust or nostalgia. It all felt the same. A look at the front door she had stepped through for the first time yesterday reminded her that she **was**n't recently accustomed to feeling at all. Her teeth tapped against each other through the spoonful of applesauce.

34

His name **was** Sun King.

Formed in the
eclipse of a record obscuring that
shining plasma eye in the sky, an abbey road to a sky
of
diamonds, or, in
angrier years, a
stairway to heaven, a highway to hell.
He knew how to
churn the hours into gold with the
turning of vinyl,
needle articulating all those notes,
bestowing corrupt knowledge, making naysayers of the
children.
Oh, it **was** just Luke

and me

and such naivety.

We **were** sitting on my bedroom floor, all immaculate handwriting and high hopes, filling out our college applications. To all the same universities, of course, lest we **be** separated, the day torn from the night, disaster unfurling to **be** as large as the distance that divided us. We didn't talk about what would happen if we got in to different schools and we didn't foresee other possibilities, the actual future, my reactional temperament. I **am** *makyo*. I **am** one who can so easily wrought destruction.

And we didn't talk about my envious temperament. He didn't notice the green in my black dark eyes, the cold grasp of jealousy snatching all warmth from them.

Because I did notice the ease with which he ticked his boxes with such strong and confident checks, how he didn't falter at the statement – *check one*.

I left the race indication section empty. I would get back to it.

One summer day, my dad took the day off to take Luke and me to the coast, with beach umbrellas and the picnic basket my mother packed all laid out in the car trunk. By the time we got there, it **was** already lunch time.

When we unwrapped the *onigiri* one gust of wind threw grains of sand into the grains of rice so each bite **was** grit grinding against the white enamel of my teeth. My dad just had to spit it out and shake his head and tell us not to go anywhere. He got us ice cream sandwiches for lunch instead.

And in our grins, the grit all faded away into the rest of the glory of our day.

We spent hours running in and out of the surf, back and forth on that stretch of beach, under the reign of the sun and under the break of our umbrella. We spent hours splashing and gleefully shrieking at the shiver-cold sea water. I spent hours smiling until my face couldn't help but hurt. I spent all of these hours until time seemed like a worthless currency and life **was** not a price to pay, and if it **was**, it should be paid in the silver of ice cream sandwich wrapping.

And as the sun set, the sun graciously ceding the earth to the night, my face started to smooth from smile to its well-learned solemnity.

And as we made our way inland, the crescent moon cackled at me and even the crisp air washing in through the open car window couldn't keep my skin from feeling hot.

When we pulled into the driveway, the house light ticked on and I saw the extent of the flush of red breaking out, burn exerting itself over the full expanse of my skin, already peeling at the shoulders. I trudged up to the front door, feeling the hot skin behind my knees stretch with every step.

I had forgotten to apply sunscreen.

Luke and Dad had both applied it evenly across their pale skin, but I didn't realize that I **was** one who would have to.

My mother looked up from her arm chair in the living room when the front door creaked open, revealing my new streaks of flaming skin. And despite it all, the grimace on my face, my rash-red skin, my mother just sighed at me.

"My white baby."

The fun and the frenzy of the day deflated at those words.

My father **was** the one who procured the aloe vera and smeared it on me to scare the cracking crimson skin away.

I'm in a navy trench coat instead of a *kimono* and

Oh no

Wouldn't it **be** cooler to **be** wrapped in cotton but I
forgot the word for-

(And I forgot the word for disgrace)

It's a *yukata*.

I remember.

Strange

What I remember.

_____

I forgot

I danced on my daddy's feet.

Every iteration of my memory **is** screwed incomplete I
forgot *obon* dancing,

The threshing suite.

Taking rain-drop sticky rice, pressing, pounding into
mochi

I forget

I forgot

_____

One night, when Luke **was** sleeping over, my mom timidly *taiko* tapped on my bedroom door. She beckoned us out into the night with her. I thought it **was** a ceremonial proceeding for the suburban stars, but as I squinted out into the dull night she asked me what I **was** looking for. I said the big and little dipper. She shook her head no, the back and forth so deliberate and weary.

She said: "In a robe of black, the stars all shine for nothing, but the moon calls us."

And she pointed to the moon with a kind of bow for reverence and to speak down to us. She told us that the rabbit **was** the noblest animal, because of its sacrifice. Sacrifice. That it would throw itself into the fire for a beggar's sake, for the purity of its heart. That **was** sacrifice. That **was** what the lunar gleam in my mother's eyes told me I was incapable of. I quaked beneath the vastness of my mother's unspoken words.

We went inside and fried *mochi*, Luke smiled with his impossibly sticky face, unstruck by what **was** and **was**n't said. I knew I didn't deserve it. My mother tisked and took what was left uneaten on my plate to the kitchen. She cleaned my dish in silence.

We set up the portable record player in the attic above the garage. We pulled up the ladder and put down the needle. The space **was** void of light, save the spring evening creeping in through the ventilation holes.

I leaned back into the intro to *Paint It, Black*. My head found a home on the dusty particle board floor. Too close to the ceiling insulation for comfort. Home **is** not comfort. I inhaled two tall shots worth of whiskey straight from the bottle. My dad **was**n't in the kind of state to notice anything missing from his liquor cabinet. He **was**n't in the kind of state to miss anything much except for my mom.

My face **was** radiating enough heat to turn the attic into a furnace. Like my mom's face would **be**. A retaliation to alcohol or a response to dark liquor. A response to drowning sorrow – a burning, a yearning for things impossible. That ill-content, that lack of acceptance. That **is** *makyo*. I felt that burning, itching to cry. It **was** in every square inch of my body, just behind the hot skin, this shivering cold. This buried hyperventilation.

But it **was** just steady breathing. Tears that didn't even know how to well. Loss that would never learn how to **be** felt. A girl that never knew how to **be** whole.

I took another swig.

I wanted to paint it black. But it **was** just feeling. It was not black, it **was** not void, it **was** whirling, swirling color and I **was** dizzy and my cheeks burn red and I couldn't help but feel, feel, feel.

I raised the bottle up to my mouth, but Luke took it from me this time. I licked the residual liquid from my lips.

It had a nice sting.

41

The record player had a bad skip.

I couldn't feel myself.

When she entered the house, it **was** already creaking and cracking without even the push and swell of the oncoming thunderstorm. The first thing her gaze latched onto, before any of the flat-cushioned couches or ring-stained tables, **was** her missing poster on the refrigerator. She threw off her back pack and walked right up to it, looked herself in the eye. The grainy black and white portrayed her tight-lipped smile, the adolescent jadedness in her eyes slanted toward the camera.

She had tracked the farm road mud in on her shoes, across the living room, to the spot where she now stood and her trench coat was damp with the misty night, but she just transfixed herself there.

He pointed to a tall stack of papers on the kitchen counter. "Those were the last ones he printed off. And there's maybe a hundred more old ones Luke had made that I put up with the other stuff in the attic." He looked at her looking at herself. They stood completely motionless, blank-faced, emotionless.

She turned her head to him slowly, looking at him just over her shoulder. "Luke, **is** he- **Is** Luke here?"

He shook his head at her. "He won't be here for another two weeks. When the term finishes. He was only here to… to take care of things." He tried to punctuate the unsavory subject matter with a smile, but his skin stretched so unnaturally.

She turned to face him fully, her trench coat wafting on the air in her spin. "Can I stay? Just until he comes back." The question resounded with such desperation. She dropped her voice. "I need to talk to him."

He nodded and she smiled something a little better than her photo, a little better than his attempt.

She looked back at the poster on the fridge.

How strange

It **is**

To **be**

Missing from a place you've never **been**. To **be**

Missing a chance to leave before the storm Morphs

Into the *taiko* drum, the *obon*

It **is** strange the things you do and don't remember. I don't remember what I had been doing before Luke came into my room that day. I don't remember who threw the first petty insult, or most of the content of the chaos that unfolded afterward.

I do remember how it felt, each comment driving feet and meters between us until even screaming couldn't bridge the difference. Until my words could only be delivered by bomb dropping.

"Just tell me I**'m** a fuck up."

I remember how far away he felt after I said that. The disconnected moment as we looked at each other, signing the final split, only happening in that instant despite all our differences, our final destination, and he **was** far away. When all I wanted was for him to **be** there, despite me pushing him away. All I wanted was to **be** in his arms, to **be** in someone's comfort, in someone's care. I just wanted to **be** someone loved.

And I remember that **was** the first day in the weeks since it happened that I had worn eyeliner and mascara again. I had been so confident that I wouldn't cry that day.

I remember looking in the mirror and encountering the proof of my error, black soot smudging down in tear lines, dirtying my pale moon face.

I remember standing in front of that mirror and wondering what I had said, what I had done. I remember wondering if there **was** anywhere left for me to go. The answer was yes. Because nowhere **was** home and anywhere **was** better if it helped me forget that I had to live in my own skin.

Really, I set out here to **be** reasonable. Maybe even apologize. But definitely at least offer my side of things.

I saw what you wrote in the newspaper. I saw how fraught and fragile you must feel. I saw it even behind the condolence flowers of your words. I could only imagine how this must **be** for you. Even though you**'re** much better at losing things, or maybe you**'re** better at having them, at knowing that you really have them. He **was** like a father to you too. Or in any case, you **were** like his sun –sorry- son. You might have even cried for him, cried like him, long soggy demonstrations of your devotion. You **were** good at being a good thing, a real pure white instead of the mix of a gritty mess of me. You **were** good at writing him to rest with that obituary, that one last calling out for me. And you **were** good at staying. Almost as good as I **was** at leaving, without a word, into the night where I belong.

Your brother tells me about those weekends you spent with my dad, pasting my black and white face all around town, until you had gone to every lamp post, every bulletin board. Your brother tells me that sometimes you and Dad would get frozen treats afterward to help take off some of the sting. You were always there to help with the sting, with ice cream or whiskey.

Yeah, your brother tells me a lot of things.

And so I fucked him.

Really, I came to explain, now how can I explain-

That the day got

T   o   r   n

From the night

I can't

remember

the last time I woke up for the day. I can't

remember

daylight, but, god, he**'s** so smooth and slow and silent
until the tear and moan.

I can explain I can't explain

    She **was** sitting on the kitchen counter watching him
wash the dishes, the steak juices off into the drain.
They could still hear the persistent beat of rain
drumming against the roof. He finished putting the
plates in the drying rack and wiped his hands with the
coarse kitchen towel. She gave him an eyes-wandering
smile. He put the towel on the counter beside her and
placed the other hand on the counter to her other side,
his body grazing her knees. He slid his hand up her
thigh, under her skirt, his hands still cold from the sink
water. A reverberation went up her spine, causing her
to extend her neck toward the rain beat roof. He pressed
his lips against it, first so light, then extracting, biting
pleasure into her pale skin.

His other hand worked up to the small of her back, then back under her shirt, unclasping her bra. She opened up her legs, kicked her heels behind his back, leaned forward to unbuckle his belt. Her wet underwear came off. His pants went down. There **was** emptiness then moaning then clawing then cumming and they laid on the kitchen floor, for a moment gasping, satisfied, but also knowing they would need more and she thought about the back pack in the foyer and what **was** inside and her insides felt full and loose and vapid.

How **am** I supposed to explain that?

Fuck me.

In the cloak of the night,

I **am** so delightless,

Ranting until someone hears me

Until the rabbit in the moon Hops back to Earth

And bites me

In a robe of black,

I **am** so comfortless,

Sparkling until someone sees me

Until the man in the moon

Smiles charmlessly

And smites me

My dad had told me that two boys **were** moving in down the street. I watched their moving truck so eagerly, the boxes and people moving in and out and back and forth.

"They might be some new friends." He suggested.

And I didn't have the omnipresence to tell him how much more than that they'd **be**, how they would become like a friend and brother or like a fuck of a lover.

About a week later, my dad invited them by. The older one was at football practice, but the one my age accepted the invitation. My dad played us his old records, every group he used to love.

"You'll like this one."

And we heard it – that one song, and both the boy and I fell in love.

Here comes the Sun King.

I don't know how many more times we went around Abbey Road together, but we kept spinning until the boy became Luke and Luke became my best friend and my best friend became a sun.

*Everyone **is** laughing. Everyone **is** happy.*

We didn't know how much we could hurt.

I hurt. I hurt I hurt I hurt. I **am** hurt. Notice me hurting. I **am** hurting. I **am** hurt.

After four days and four nights, she stalked off to the foyer, returning with the black back pack. She sat in the sag in the sofa. Both of them **were** colored by the lightning flashes of commercial images. The sound of the zipper **was** muted by the volume of the TV, turned up to tune out the beats of rain on the tin porch roof.

She drew out a plastic gallon bag, fit to pop with cocaine and he just raised his eyebrows, not inquiring as to how she had come to acquire such a quantity.

He **was**n't one to ask questions.

She **was**n't one to offer explanations.

She took a credit card out of the bag's front pocket and cut up two lines each for the both of them, the pure white of it neatly illuminated by the TV instead of the waxing moon.

It took the edge off of waiting. Soon the lines would seem endlessly long. Soon it would all **be** gone.

I stopped taking my shoes off in the house. I liked the sound of my footsteps proclaiming my presence as a warning. *Stop crying, Father.* Yes, their dirt crashed against the floor as if to say, *your soggy demonstrations defile her legacy of silence. That quiet, so much like her that she seemed to embody it, so potent that we continue unwrapping it in and with her absence. Stop paving over it with your sobs.*

He would stand in the kitchen over a can of Campbell's chicken noodle soup for dinner. I would hear the uneven breathing of his lungs leaking out their last expressions of love. He had to live that pain, but I had to hear it.

I started wearing Docs, big, bulky, noisy things, and wearing them from the moment I woke up. I would clack around the house from the crack of dawn. The shoes would speak for me. *Good morning. Notice me. Please stop crying.* The shoes would spit in the face of my mother's ghost. There **was** no face left to save.

And when I felt I **was**n't enough to fill my own shoes, I stopped my drum feet performance and let my dad soak stain the sacrosanct silence with his soggy sobbing sounds. I started my regular tip-toe procession to his liquor cabinet, knowing even the empty bottles wouldn't **be** loud enough in their cry. *Notice me. I, like her, need to **be** someone loved.*

I dreamed that the curtains **were**n't closed last night and the rain storm stopped looming over me. So when high noon hit, a stray beam of light fell over my fast-asleep face.

It felt so nice.

Like fingers reaching out to tenderly stroke my cheek, tell me it**'s** all okay. But if it**'s** Luke, then the fingers would **be** pointing, accusatory, shame, shame.

Because what the hell **am** I doing in his brother's bed? And who **am** I to think anyone will tell me it**'s** okay?

I hope he comes back soon, while I still have the mind to try to explain.

It **was** the first and only time my father and I went camping. It **was** just me and him and now I can't remember why. I can't remember where Luke **was**, what circumstances miraculously separated us.

We drove out of the suburban limits, watching the dense housing disperse into the dry dust of the countryside. My eyes wandered off into the unpolluted expanse of it all. My dad's eyes turned forward to the rugged concrete of the road.

My mother didn't even pack any food to take, no rations of rice to go along with us. He denied all her attempts and instead insisted that we would eat hot dogs all weekend. Roasting hot dogs over a fire, he repeated over and again, that **was** camping. None of this *bento* box, pansy food-packing bullshit.

By the time we finished pitching the tent it **was** already well into the early autumn night. He worked away at trying to build a fire in the dark while I in shivered in my thin sweatshirt. It sparked small and he couldn't for the life of him coax it to get any bigger, despite his encouragement turned bitter grumbling.

Eventually he gave up and we cooked the hot dogs, slowly, painstakingly, over a match like fire. He didn't have a guitar or anything to talk about with me, so he just hummed to himself.

And before we went into our tent for the night, Dad pointed up to the moon. "You see the man?"

I quirked my head, puzzled.

"No? You've never noticed him before?" He bent down to my level, pointing to the man's characterizing craters. "There, that big crater more to the left, that's one eye. And then the other crater is the other eye. He's kind of squinting. Can you see him?"

I looked at my father, squinting up at the sky, so desperate to have me see the proper shape, to have the moon become his mirror. He **was** so adamant, so asinine silly that I searched for the man too. And after a minute or two, in that strange interpretive hide-and-seeking, I found him. I told my dad, giggling, excited. He chuckled at me and went into the tent.

But as I gazed up at the moon, there **was** a switch and I only saw the nose-twitching, self sacrificing, *mochi*-pounding creature. I blinked. The man **was** back, gazing off into the night abyss that surrounded him. Then his cheek **was** the rabbit, still there, diligently. The shift between them, so rapid, so dizzying so I couldn't decide what I saw. I couldn't tell what would **be** next. It **was** just the moon, moments ago so sublimely peaceful as it presided over the starry sky. Now it **was** a conflict zone, a tug-of-war, a back-and-forth, a push-and-pull and it pulled me apart.

I went into the tent and buried myself in the sleeping bag.

We **were** sitting on the floor in my room upstairs. We heard the thump. Just one fell thump and an accompanying kitchen clatter. My mother soared to the floor. Her heart, shattered. It would come to **be** known as the heart attack. I wish it **was** called what it **was**: heart stop, heart shatter, soul scatter.

My mother had ceased in her perfection performance.

I knew it **was** a mistake even as I was doing it. Of course I did. I knew it **was** a mistake far before he yelled it at me that day. I could see through it, through myself. I might have even seen what would become of my unthinking actions, the fallout of the fight, my disappearing into the night.

I took the college applications out into the back yard, under the reign of the full moon, and destroyed them one by one. All those papers, unsent. All those years of preparation, unfulfilled. Like some kind of ritual, like something spiritual, like my mom would look down from the heavens, at the fire, nose twitching.

But instead, there **was** no crying out, no one to stop me, so I turned my dreams to ash. I **am** *makyo*. I **am** one to wrought destruction. I **am** one to give into the storm of desire.

I	will	burn	in	this		flood.
Rain		**Is**		scalding.		
I		**Am**		balling.		
I		**Am**		sobbing.		
I	will	drown	in	this	fire.	
Rain		**Is**		fire.		
Everything		**Is**		burning.		
Everything		**Is**		rattling.		

This	house		**is**	quake.
This	house		**is**	shake.
Every	thing		**is**	wrong.

I   **Am**   sorry.
I   **Am**   atrocious.
I   **Am**   scared.

This   house   **is**   burning.
This   house   **is**   yearning.
This   house   **is**

Can   I   go   back?

I   **Am**   sorry.
I   **Am**   strange.
I   **Am**   the moon.

But I **am** afraid of the dark.

My mom's porcelain *Hakata* doll soars to the floor. Her face, jagged pieces.

No more smooth pure white.

Her face ceases in its lunar performances. No more shining.

No more slanted eyes.

No more perfect white skin.

She called me

her beautiful white flower.

I **am** a breaker.

I **am** white.

I **am** her beautiful white flower.

She loves me. She loves me not. She loves me. She loves me –

It**'s** not

that I wanted to break it.

I wanted to **be** it and

I couldn't

and I couldn't stand it

I've locked myself up here with the rest of my parents'
things In the

Attic

In a

Panic

Going going going gone.

—

I'**m** sorry, Mom,

(For breaking your doll). I'**m** sorry, Dad,

(For snapping your records). I'**m** learning how to cry
Like you taught me.

Learning how to die

Like you taught me.

But you never taught me.

You never taught me how

To live.

You never taught me how To love,

Except for

In silence or

In sobbing.

You never taught me how To love

All

myself.

I **was**

So empty

That

I filled myself

With:

His brother,

Cocaine.

Not in a *yukata* and Shame

Shame

Shame

Shame

I'm gone From this House.
I'll
Descend The three Floors.
I gotta
Get out. Float
Out?
The rabbit Ascended. It would Throw
Itself.
I will
Throw
Myself.
I will
Be
Full.
Like
The moon.
Did you call me?
I
'
m
G
o
n
e
.

I
L
e
f
t

.

I
'

m
S
o
r
r
y

.

She ran down the stairs. The two flights. She spun past where he had **been** beating at the floor, at the attic door. She threw herself past the back pack and empty gallon bag. She threw herself out the front door. She threw herself out into the night, the rain finally stopped, and rushed out to the full moon hanging in the now cloudless sky over the field. She slid and slopped and sobbed until she **was** a heap on the ground. She bowed down to the two-faced moon, trying to save herself, her own face.

She peaked back up. The moon had vanished. The clear sky spat black where its luminous shape would **be**.

The moon **was** vacant.

Chop   *chop*   *chop*   With   a   credit   card.

Pound   *pound*   *pound*   With   a   mochi
pallet.

Chop   *pound*   ***bang***   Blood   ***splatter***.

Pound   *chop*   brain   ***Bam***   mush.

Bam   ***pound***   ***Chop***   Guts   ***gush.***

         Sweet   White   Silent   *shush.*

Explosions   ended.

Just   a   Juicy   Organ   rush.

She**'s** just a pulp to cradle.

I heard the rabbit and the man

Held hands

When they smashed what **was** left of her into moon
craters.

April Full Moon Special

Nature's Embrace

Hasib Iftekhar

(An ode to all the ones battling hopelessness)

The hustling in the trees, & carrying of the breeze,
They do speak to me.
And a whisper so droll, a bow to the bole,
Wheezes out in silence:
'Keep on keeping on, and don't let go'.

Rile across the skin, with an agony to the bone -
I twitch and look up between all the moans,
In a weary body and dragging head,
I attempt to look farther,
As my frame sinks further -
Ninety-nine days of frozen still,
in my lone infirmary bed.

Isolation, ventilation, so dreadful is the prohibition!
Smacked down I am by nauseating preconditions.
In desolation, meandering thoughts are what I mime -
to a reflection on the dusk window: my audience.
Leave room out there in the pane for Melancholy,
To stain the glass a gloomy purple.

Mornings though, shines through hope,
To a rancid soul that struggles to cope.
Leaves swoosh in with songbirds chirping,
Hops me back alive & retorting.

And the sky, o my! Such cerulean frame.
Dots of cotton – a broom there? Or button?
From here to Serengeti, via the eternity,
So grand & so big, puts a Renoir to shame.

And I sense the vitals soar & goosebumps appear,
Cracks turning fade and demons steer clear.

On there a plateau, I lay flat and serene,
As evened-out as I could ever be.
The kindness amongst all things I feel,
Stoking a bliss within me.

Blood Vessels

Lauren Klein

At last, they had finally found the source of the pain. It was something in his lung, some blood vessels that had dried completely and turned hard and brittle. On the x-ray slide, it looked like a spindly branch from a bare tree had been shoved inside his left lung. As he breathed in and out, he fancied he could feel the points of the twigs pressing against the inside of his chest, like wires plugged into nothing. The doctor spoke in a low voice as he traced his index finger over the spidery map of Sturgis's lung and pointed out the problem area, where the lines showed up much darker than the rest. Eventually, they would crumble and turn to dust. Acute Pulmonary Venial Solidifinosis was the official name.

There were several treatment options.

"The first is to do nothing," the doctor said. He was an even-tempered fellow with graying hair, manicured fingernails, and the suggestion of a fading spray tan. Superficial, easy-going, and competent. "You can wait until the veins dry up and crumble and then have the dust vacuumed out of your lung with a small surgical tube, or just sneeze it out. Both would be very painful. And your lung could collapse. I wouldn't recommend this option.

"The second is to have them removed and replaced with some wires, like the kind that come out of the back of your VCR, and hope that they will merge with the rest of your veins in time. The only problem is that sometimes the plastic can create a buildup of toxins in the body, which can lead to cancer, although the research is still preliminary.

"The third is to cut out the solidified parts of the veins and have glass tubes inserted to make the blood flow as it is supposed to, but this technology is experimental and, if you choose this route, you have to severely restrict your movements. If, for example, someone knocks into you on the bus, the tubes could burst and the insides of your lung would be filled with shards of glass. If that happened, your entire lung might seize up from the pain and we would have to remove it completely to get all the glass out. And then we may not be able to put it back in."

The doctor advised him to think about it and let him know in two weeks. Sturgis buttoned his shirt, put on his jacket, and left the hospital. He was dismayed. He hoped that this pain, which had been gnawing with progressive ferocity over the past months, would turn out to be a muscle injury, or something that would heal itself, but this was much more complicated.

The doctor said that years of heavy smoking had probably sped up the solidification process. But Sturgis thought the real cause must be his own cold-heartedness, his refusal to let any emotion flow through his body, all the years of unexpressed sentiment that had finally dried up inside him, pumped from a heart so arthritic and reptilian that it could no longer support both lungs.

A prune-like man in a hospital gown tossed his cigarette into the bushes nearby and shoved past Sturgis with his walker, the IV he trailed after himself knocking into the automatic door as it tried to close. Sturgis realized he had been blocking the entrance to the hospital. The sliding doors kept trying to shut, coming close to him, hesitating, and opening again, repeatedly.

He breathed the cold spring air, which smelled distinctly medical, surveyed the dirty snow melting into the sides of the building, and decided, despite the pain, to walk all the way home. As he set off down the sidewalk, he thought about what he would tell Vivian.

Truthfully, he wasn't sure how she would react, if she reacted at all. She was no longer the prim, anxious Vivian he had fallen in love with. Over the past two years, she had grown wild, loud, and crass. She had started wearing tight leopard-print pants and lacy red push-up bras. When she wasn't spending her days–and sometimes even entire nights– at her friend Lina's, she would stay on the phone with her for hours, winding the cord around herself while she cooked or cleaned the kitchen in her new sequined slippers, chatting and laughing so loudly he could hear her from the study upstairs.

"Why don't you invite her over then?" he suggested once, partly as a way to get her to stop running up the phone bill and partly out of curiosity about this Lina character. Vivian scowled and muttered something about a far distance.

"That's why I end up spending the night sometimes," she explained. But after enough cajoling, she agreed. She had no reason not to, and she knew it.

As it turned out, Lina lived ten minutes away. After much anticipation, she arrived on the appointed day in a black lace dress with an enormous bouquet of lilacs. She and Vivian shrieked when they greeted each other, like they were sisters finally meeting after years apart, and touched each other's clothes and hair affectionately. Watching them, Sturgis wished Vivian would still touch him like that. It had been so long now.

Most likely, he just wouldn't tell her, or their daughter, who was away at college. At least not yet. He would wait until he had figured out what to do. She had been on the phone when he told her he was going to the doctor, his voice shaking, his trembling fingers struggling to button his coat. "Uh-huh," she nodded. She would probably still be on the phone when he got back, having failed to register that he had even left. He pictured her sitting at the kitchen table with a cup of tea in front of her, playing with the phone cord, smiling. "I have pulmonary fucking solidifinosis," he would tell her. "The veins in my lung are rock-hard. There's not much they can do," and she would just nod with her eyes glazed over and immediately the pain would intensify and he would have to sit down.

He was feeling weak now. The main avenue seemed endless and he wanted to flag down one of the buses, but he didn't want to run to catch it. Why were the blocks so long, why were there so many trees obscuring the sky with their twisting fingers? When it came time to cross, he had to jog across the wide avenue to get to the other side in time. He felt angry that the amount of time allotted by the crosswalk was clearly dangerous for the old and infirm and resolved to write a letter to city council full of bitter complaints.

He was entering his neighbourhood now, a quiet corner of the south end. There was still so far to go and the pain was getting worse. He considered sitting down for a few minutes, but the benches he passed in the park were wet and he didn't want to get mud on his nice corduroys, so he kept going, slowly winding his way through the damp streets.

The house sat at the end of a wide, sleepy road. As he made his way towards it he hoped that maybe, by some miracle, she would be off the phone by the time he got home and would make him a sandwich and a warm brandy. The thought was so tantalizing that as he turned the corner towards the house, he almost believed it was possible.

They weren't on the phone anymore. Lina was here, in his kitchen, sitting in his wife's lap and kissing her passionately. Their limbs were intertwined. One of Lina's purple high-heeled shoes had fallen off and was lying on the linoleum. The kettle was whistling on the stove. They didn't stop when he walked in. They seemed totally oblivious.

He turned the burner off and stood there watching them, the pain in the left side of his chest throbbing more intensely than ever, as if his twig-like veins were finally about to snap. He wondered why the doctor had recommended lung treatments when clearly his heart was the source of the problem, broken and defective as it was. He could feel it swelling painfully right now. It must have been a misdiagnosis. At his next appointment he would request–no, demand–extensive heart scans, Electronic Cardiograms, blood tests for everything. He remembered some kind of test where they measure your heartbeat against a hamster running on a wheel. He would ask for that too, and whatever else the suave doctor had to offer.

But now, confronted with the abundant lust of his wife and her best friend, he felt an enormous weariness. He took his coat off and wandered into the living room. On the t.v screen, a stylized action movie was playing. A man had been shot and was falling in slow motion through the air, emitting a vibrant jet of blood. Close up shots showed the blood splashing gloriously, the luscious crimson of pagan times, the warm gushing of life, as the man's body crashed to the ground and his eyes bulged. Sturgis switched off the t.v and went upstairs to lie down.

Assimilation

Marina Lopez

a menudo nos repetimos
> we often repeat ourselves

para quienes solo oyen música en nuestra lengua
materna
> for those who only hear music in our mother tongue

para nuestros hijos
> for our children

para quienes somos extranjeros
> for whom we are foreigners

para nuestros amores
> for our loves

quienes nunca nos conocerán de lleno
> who will never fully know us

para nuestros abuelos
> for our grandparents

que no nos reconocen
> that do not recognize us

nos repetimos
> we repeat ourselves

en sueños
> in dreams

notando cómo perdemos el hilo
> noting how we are losing the thread

notando que nos estamos diluyendo
> realizing we are becoming diluted

sin rostro
> faceless

sin venas
> veinless

sin raíces

                                    rootless

nos repetimos

                             we repeat ourselves

esperando que algo de nuestra esencia

                         hoping some of our essence

quede

                                   remains

Marina Lopez, 2021-2022

an exercise in empathy

Marina Lopez

I am your mother
father
brother
sister
aunt
uncle you stopped talking to

I am a good person
I believe this is a good land
I believe we are a good people

and all that is evil is held
within a cabal of monsters
so that the world makes sense

or maybe my soul has scars that never healed
shellshocked, I stumble unto your newsfeed

if only

you could breathe my yearning
for a time lost
a time to be proud of

it would crush your chest
with longing

if only

you could taste my pain
acrid, it would scab your tongue
it would corrode your mouth in words of dead dreams

you cannot speak
dreams of supremacy
or dreams of revolution
or dreams of simply getting by

you look at me
through this digital funhouse that gapes
between us like the red sea

my features distorted
my eyes wilder and sorrier
more menacing
and more familiar
than they actually might be

am I
a figment of your imagination?

am I
you

staring hours on end,
doom-scrolling
through this well,

drowning
blinded by your reflection

unable to see me unable to see you
unable to touch me unable to touch you
unable to speak me unable to speak you

this apathetic arachnid nurses us
in an algorithm optimizing engagement

and you
in your perilous cocoon
reach out to me
stretching, stretching
unable to grasp the face
behind the many masks
at the bottom of this bottomless well

Marina Lopez, 2020-2022

To love a man

Marina Lopez

in 1900
to bare him a child of forgiveness
after he gives your sister a child of betrayal

or to love a man

in 1950
a man that beats you
demands his meals
and banishes you from the table

or to love a boy

in 2010
who can't square your brain with your body
and so insists on denying your womanhood

To love a man
when the world insists you should
or when the world insists you shouldn't

to love a person

to love the moments when the gaze opens
and you can see the soul behind the man-mask

to crave and to hope
that the man-mask shatters

or to be unable to imagine the man-mask's death
and to still love the man

to be denied your story
by a future that insists
that the only men worth loving
are men that don't yet exist

to hope and to crave
that the man-mask shatters

to be proven right
when the boy grows into a man
who sees you

to be proven wrong
when the man serenades your sister at the convent
he put her in

to never truly know
whether the man can walk, talk, breathe
without his mask

Marina Lopez 2021

April's 2nd New Moon Special

Tantric

William E. Heston

In the kitchen,
Bodhidharma and I sit,
     A bucket of gas station fried chicken
     Split between us.

     "The world is at its end," I tell him.
"What do we do
When we've lost our moral center?
When without breath,
     the walls begin to hyperventilate
     In rhythm with our chests?"

He eats,
Crumbs tumbling down the front of his robe,
Tea leaf eyelids hung
     In perpetual rest.
He smiles at me.

"What do we do
When time unravels?" I ask.
"When String Theory unwinds;
When the stairs go
     Nowhere?"

Still, he sits,
        Cross-legged on the linoleum,
        Slopping up the greasy skin
Of a drumstick.

"Bodhidharma, I'm tired, and, frankly, disgusted.
The stench of grief hangs on the breath
                Of dead dreams
        That used to call to us.
How am I supposed to answer them?
How do YOU suppose I answer?"

He rubs his single bare foot,
        Picks at the sandal on the other,
        And I wait with a festering sense of impatience.

The evening sun disappears from my back window,
        Receding into the urban overgrowth
        Of the yard.

        "We're at war!" I exclaim,
"Why are we without territory this time?
Why are we fighting
        Simply to maintain the line?
How senseless can the ends get
If there's always a means to defend them?

I need answers.
I don't trust you're here.

Who else
Do I have left?"

He drops the bone in the bucket.
He grabs his staff to stand,
        The missing sandal hung atop.
He turns to me

And asks
"Why?"

gluttony

Mackenzie Macrol

in my room, there is a box full of memories from a time when i was at my worst in everything. in that box is a pair of leggings reserved for when i reached my final goal. i have never worn that pair of leggings. every season, my target weight would lower. and lower. and lower. people began to tell me they worried that a strong autumn wind would blow me over, but the leggings stayed in the box because i remained terrified that they wouldn't fit. i think that's the thing people don't understand about gluttony. nothing is ever enough.

ghost

Mackenzie Macrol

i can't help but be sad for her, y'know?
i cannot help but grieve
and i see her out there
in a sea of stranger's faces
and i think the ghost of her is me

May Full Moon Special

message in a bottle

Mackenzie Macrol

the other day, i found a message in a bottle on the beach. water had seeped in from the cracks and holes in the cork meant to seal it, and the ink had been almost completely washed away. i consider the hundreds of thousands of miles of open ocean and foolishly think that i've never felt that kind of desperation—where your final call for help could very well drown with you. then, i remember the hands that held me back. surrounding me, deceiving me, their touches sustained pressure, like a dive in the open ocean. as a reward for my complacency, i was promised mercy below the surface. i was promised that the choppy waves above this still, open ocean were too dangerous for a breath of fresh air. i was promised that without the anchor they created, i would lose my direction. i was promised that i would more likely drown trying to swim against the current. so, I sank—saltwater filled my lungs and made a hundred thousand cuts, killing me from the inside out. when i eventually realized that i'd been made to drown, my first cries for help were hardly waterproof.

The Thing About Being a Poet

Ris V. Rose

The thing about being a poet
Is that you don't just decide one day
To be a poet.
That isn't how it works.
It isn't something you can simply dabble in;
It's an all-consuming
Omnipotent
Omniscient
Calling,
A command
From some higher power.
The thing about being a poet
Is that once you start,
You can never stop—
It is an emotional commitment
To looking at the world a certain way
No matter the personal toll—
A commitment
You did not have the choice to make.

But the thing about being a poet
That no one is willing to talk about
Is the deep
Fundamental
Permanent
Irreparable
Aching sadness
Woven into your DNA,
Clawing at anything
It can get its hands on,
Waiting in the background like a ghost
Or the shadow of two people

Holding hands
Stretching behind you on the sidewalk.
It's the only thing
We cannot seem to put into words.

-Ris
June 2020
Because do you think we WANT to look up at the stars
and start crying?

A Lovely Word

Ris V. Rose

"Poet" is such a lovely word
For someone who turns other people
Into villains,
Someone who can only express their emotions
Through written word
Because they have no control
Over their voice,
Someone who masks their feelings,
Their malicious intentions,
Mascara stains,
The light switch on
At three in the morning,
And their fixations—
Even on things that happened
Before the poet became Poet—
Under the guise of art,
Someone who wakes from nightmares
That one day
Their name will not be painted
On bookstore walls
Because,
Beneath the pretty words,
The surfeit of documents,
The ink stains on their hands,
And the smile on their face,
"Poet" is a lovely word
For someone who doesn't believe in themselves.

-Ris
March 2021
I'll be saying goodbye soon. To both. Ouch.

It's Okay

Ris V. Rose

I. She stands before me,
    A young girl,
    Maybe five years old,
    And looks up at me,
    Expecting me to say something—
    Because isn't that what adults do:
    Talk
    And expect you to listen?
    I get down on my knee,
    Wrap her in a hug,
    And whisper,
    "It's okay"—

    It's okay
    That sometimes you spend so long
    Talking to your toys
    That you forget that they aren't real.
    It's okay
    That your room feels like a different place,
    Like a magic place,
    Like you could open the door
    And be in any world you wanted.

II. She stands before me,
    A young girl,
    Maybe twelve years old,
    And looks up at me,
    Expecting me to say something—
    Because isn't that what happens at school:
    Teachers talk at you all day
    And expect you to listen?
    I bend down,

Wrap her in a hug,
And whisper,
"It's okay"—

It's okay
That you really like to be alone.
It's okay that you have feelings inside
That you can't quite give names to.
It's okay that you talk to
A little man in a little tuxedo
Who sits upon your shoulder
When you walk home.
Because you feel like
There isn't anyone else
You really fit with.
It's okay that the magic world inside your head
Has only gotten bigger
And it's okay
That the pen feels good in your hand
Even though it has nothing to say
(Yet).

III. She stands before me,
     A young woman,
     Maybe seventeen years old,
     And looks straight at me,
     Expecting me to say something—
     Because isn't that what's supposed to happen
     When someone is trying to help you:
     They talk
     And you listen?
     I step toward her,
     Wrap her in a hug,
     And whisper,
     "It's okay"—

You're going to bleed
For a long time.
You're going to bury your pain
Deep down
Under straight-As
And pretty words
And pretty boys.
You're going to spend so much time
Running away from Here
That you can almost forget what Here looks like.
Almost.
You're going to look at the moon
And feel both
A, "Come home," sort of tugging,
And a, "That's not who I am anymore," sort of
repulsion.
You're going to watch roses bloom
And die
And bloom again.
But it's okay, because
The only reason I am here
To say these things to you at all
Is because of you.

IV. She stands before me,
    A woman,
    Maybe thirty years old,
    And I look at her,
    Expecting her to say something—
    Because isn't that the whole point of all this:
    To tell your younger self something
    And hope they can even hear you?
    But that isn't how life works,
    So I wrap myself in a hug
    As her image fades away
    Into the clouds

And whisper to myself,
"It's okay."

*One day you'll get there
And then you'll know exactly what she was
trying to say.*

-Ris
October 2020
*If you could tell your younger self something, what
would you say?*

May New Moon Special

The Math of Love 1+1=1

Ziaul Moid Khan

"I want to touch you," I said, looking straight into Reshma's bizarre bright eyes. In the last two weeks, this was the seventeenth time I'd asked my newly found love this question in the hope of a positive response. The last sixteen attempts of my maneuver had proved futile producing no concrete result. I was on fire, every atom of me crying desperately for her.

"You cannot," she said, and giggled like an innocent baby. Her blood red lips exposed her extra white teeth. Whiter than what they show in the toothpaste ads during those short commercial horrible breaks on television.

She was one of those rare looking girls fit for modelling, cat walk, the showbiz world. Slander, but with heavy bosom. Her tits shook heavily up and down as she walked giving a clear hint that she did not wear a bra, wittingly to draw more than usual attention.

"Why?" I said, perplexed.

"That I can't and won't tell you." She laughed again, giving me her usual response in mirth.

"Why not? Please…please Reshma, tell me!" I said pissed and pinched by her rude reply, "why do you always evade my questions, love?"

"Some other day, when the right winds will blow and bring around an opportune time," Reshma said, staring at the full moon that was trying to evade the dark clouds which were advancing towards her.

I fell silent. Looked up where she was staring—at the glittering sky. It was a perfect night with a circled moon and all galaxies of stars, adding to the beauty of the vast expense of the cosmos. We sat at our usual place—a hummock where the Krishna River flowed fifty meters below our feet. More often than not we came here after our first meeting-by-chance. Here it was peaceful, and both of us loved this place—away from the hustle and bustle of the city-life.

Last night at this same place she'd asked me if I really loved her.

"Of course, I do," I had said.

Then she'd said nothing. It seemed odd to me, but I did not nudge her lest she should be offended. A little short tempered was she. Truly I didn't want to lose her. I could not afford it.

"Are you OK, Nawaz?" she chirped. And I was back from my flashback.

"Yes. Why are you asking?"

"I guess you're hurt," she said. Her lips seemed to be the untouched petals of some new blossoming rosebud. *I want to kiss these coral lips*, I wanted to say but did not. Sometimes it's safe not to say something your heart's crying to speak aloud.

"It's not like that," I said, looking sideways, "I think I have no right upon you."

"May I ask you one thing?"

"Yes."

"Which kind of right you want by the way? You mean physical!"

"All the rights," I said with possession in my tone, "physical and platonic, both."

"Of course, you'll have, Nawaz," she said with an I-know-your-intention-smile, "but give me some time. I can feel your feelings. But as for now—all the rights are reserved."

"Take your time," I said with sarcasm in my tone.

"Thanks," she said, casually this time, with no apparent emotions in her words.

~

The cupid shot his love-infected-bloody-arrow, as I got interested in Reshma the moment I saw her. Such peace on any mortal being I'd never spotted before. She was—oval faced, big eyes, good height and white as snow albeit not as beautiful as Snow White, but enough to spell a charm on a lad like me. She spoke the minimum words possible. Most of her answers were 'Yes', 'No', 'Maybe', 'Can't Say', and sometimes a faint 'Sure.' But I got in her a temporary refuge from my joblessness.

As I remember it now, I wanted to chat more on the very first day I met her. "I've an urgent piece of work, there." She pointed into the distance, the churchyard. And then she told—there was her father's grave. Mr. Goodfellow had died in a road accident, when he was on a high and could not judge the speeding truck, coming from the opposite direction near Vijayawada. I showed my sympathy, which she did not seem to have noticed or cared for.

A week later, she introduced me to this place, a small hilltop at the outskirts of my town—dangerous but pretty-looking, just like her. She insisted to come here every evening if I wished to meet her. I had to agree. And thus, it became our regular rendezvous. She loved twilight and I loved her. So, I was always agreed, to whatever she said, willy-nilly. One thing among many things startling about her was—her hair ever seemed drenched with dripping droplets of water as if she came out of a shower right then. I wished to ask about it but did not.

I could discern the rise and fall of her sizeable bosom. The white strip of her bra was peeping through her semi-transparent top that gave me a bizarre thrill, an excitement beyond words. I wanted to touch these tits. But her feelings seemed cold and indifferent to me. The night was illumined with a bare army of stars led by the shining moon. The howling of wolves could unmistakably be heard. But they must have been at a far distance somewhere into the deep forest. I thought we were away from their reach or it could be a misconception too.

"Don't you feel afraid to come here," I said, without looking at her, for I always resisted an urge to embrace her. That was what I always wanted. And that was what she always declined.

"What should I be afraid of and why should I be afraid of?" she said, still staring at the snail-moving moon. Her voice had a chime unexplainable.

"Those wolves in the woods," I said, "aren't they horrific?"

"They are the children of night," she said, "not something to be fearful of. I love their howl. You should too."

There was silence again. Only the gurgling of the river-water, beneath, made its presence felt apart from the occasional voices of the wolves.

"Their spooky howling terrifies me," I said, drawing her attention toward my natural fear.

"That's background music, nothing beyond it. Just chill, Nawaz!"

Reshma shifted her glance from the moon to the current of Krishna River that was sprinting towards an unknown location. Every river finds its way to the ocean.

"You know swimming?" she said after a pause, looking at the tumultuous current of water fifty meters down our feet, where it formed several mini whirlpools. A fall from our place was a confirmed horrible death.

"No," I said, albeit it was a lie. I'd once been a state swimming champion, but that was years back when I was in high school. I hid this truth without any apparent reason, just to reveal it to her later. That was my weird habit—to surprise someone later by revealing the truth.

"Close your eyes," she said with a sudden glint of light in her eyes.

"Are you going to push me?" I said and cracked into laughter. The voice echoed from the woods.

"I'll save you, if you drown. Don't worry, I know swimming," she said and laughed, exposing her bare teeth again. Sometimes I felt some unknown terror when I saw two of them—her side canines—slightly longer than the rest in the set.

"Close your eyes," she repeated and chuckled. I was wedged in her charm.

Like an obedient child, I obliged this time, and felt a gentle push, at the same time, from behind. Her touch was ice-cold as if from a corpse. At first, I thought Reshma was just kidding, but realized in a few nanoseconds that I'd been literally pushed—to die—by someone I loved so intensely. Before I could calculate anything, I was airborne. The gravitational force of the earth pulled me towards the hissing waters. For a couple of seconds, I was sort of navigating in the space. I did not know when a squeak escaped my lips—*R E S H M A...!*

~

Then I heard a thunderous splash—the sound effect of my own great fall— as my chest hit against the foaming current. A terrible acute pain ran through my chest as though someone had pierced a long *Rampuri* knife into me. I writhed, convulsed in excruciating pain tinged with utter disbelief. I felt cheated, I felt deceived. I was still unable to digest the fact for being tossed into the river by someone I loved. To whom I was most likely to propose, with a red rose in hand and my left knee on the ground.

And I gulped water, a lot of water indeed, as my own painful body sank inside the devouring waters. The Krishna River was not indeed as polite as Lord Krishna (was). The water seemed to have conspired with my Girl — to kill me by drowning. Still I was unable to figure out why the hell she wanted my annihilation, and as promised she did not jump after me. I jerked. *Was her love a façade? What profit did she have of my death after all?*

But putting aside all my philosophy on love for the time being, I suddenly recalled my swimming lessons. My hands and legs mechanically moved as though remembering the old methods I'd learned in my school's swimming pool.

Somehow, I managed to come afloat on the water-surface. My fearful eyes caught a glimpse of my Girl who still sat at the hillock with her feet dangling over the fast current of the river I was drowning in. I had no time to see whether her eyes were focused on me or drifted elsewhere. It seemed irrelevant now.

I peddled and side-stroked the water with all my strength, momentarily forgetting my terrible chest pain and the double cross that my lady-love had done to me. The priority now was neither to touch her nor to embrace her and not even to see her beautiful cleavage and her tight tits that reminded me of Britney Spears, but to save my life from the awful waters.

Luckily, I could manage to swim tonight though not like a champion, for I had left my practice years back, yet at least enough to bring myself to safety. The fast river flow was, however, hampering me to make headway. To bring myself out, I was fighting against the monstrous current. But it was not that easy given the circumstances. My body seemed too weak to swim with ease.

Under the moonlight, the water looked blue, but treacherous and not at all amiable. Within a minute I realized I could not move against the great force of the entire river. *Use the current to reach the side of the river,* shouted my mind. I gave the thought a fighting chance, took a sharp U-turn and swam with the flow of the river. Cleverly, I kept striving to come up close to the bank until I felt the side wall of Krishna.

My hands clutched at something. First it was the moss, but I tried again and again and then again. Eventually I gripped at some long side-grown-grass and the deep rooted-hollow-reeds. I held fast to them and my body momentarily stabilized. I somehow crawled myself up clutching my hands at the higher reeds. I slipped thrice, but at my fourth or fifth effort, I succeeded climbing out of the hostile river. It was a welcome relief.

In my heart I thanked God besides my swimming coach Mr. Maitrey as I lay beside the river, breathing heavily on the dust-laden side path with drenched, cold, and torn clothes. I remained so for twenty minutes or so. Then I recollected all that had happened and stood up to thank my love for her attempted murder. With slow strides, I walked to the bridge, where-from was the route to the hillock she sat upon. From a distance I could see — she was still there, still staring at the full moon.

~

There I found her sitting wherefrom she had pushed me. Her clothes were gone. All. Moonlight made her look scintillating. Her tits, tight and pointing. Her v-part hidden as she lay her bony hands in her lap. Her legs bare and inviting. Any other night, I would have not waited a semi second to embrace her but tonight was different.

"Reshma," I said with rage in my eyes as I approached her, "what the hell was that? You almost killed me."

"The real life starts only after death," she said, taking a deep sigh that seemed to be a grunt as if nothing had happened. "You don't know the simple math of love; it's 1+1=1. Two bodies, but one soul," she said and giggled. Her laughter echoed in the distance. "You had to dissolve into me, if you wished to touch me or achieve me. And it was not possible unless you died or transformed."

"What the hell do you mean?" I thundered, my body still shivering, whether with cold or fury or both—I did not know.

"Relax, Nawaz Khan, relax," she said her voice extra cold, "we're from two different worlds, you know. I think you don't know. What you call life is short lived, miserable and what you call death is—a stone reality, long and eternal. You call it life—the filthy world you live in. I was only trying to fulfill your desire—to touch me or make love with me, but perhaps Providence wants your presence more in the human world and least in ours—the cold world of Thin Airs."

I fumbled for the right words as I froze. Again, whether it was the effect of her stunning revelation that suddenly dawned upon me or the cold river water—still dripping off my clothes, I did not know. But I stood baffled, out-of-my-wits and unable to speak as she made her lips round and whistled weirdly.

By now my love for her—for reasons unknown to me—had ceased substantially. The deep desire to take her into my arms was no longer there. The fever of love, that appeared earlier to be an eternity, was over. The threat of death made somehow drastic changes in my approach. But still I stood there confounded, my teeth rattling, while my shocked eyes gazing her in utter disbelief, as she whistled again, this time clearer than before. What was she doing? Soon, I got the answer.

~

The dense forest had a sudden ruckus as if in response to her whistling. The thorns and hedges shivered like in a storm and came to a sudden animation, and then there appeared from nowhere before us—a big pack of wolves. My words froze in my mouth—surrounded by 40-50 wolves was a new experience to me. Every moment it felt like they'd attack on me and tear me apart. Reshma stood up from her place and walked elegantly to them—like a princess towards her minions—and waved them to remain calm. But their blood red flaming eyes were still staring at me like they were waiting for orders from their mistress.

"We could be one, but alas we could not," she said, looking into my eyes and rubbing the neck of one of wolves that stood close in obedience to its mistress, "it's a pity that to my virgin love you could not enjoy. No need to fear now, live your life. Anyway, good bye Nawaz!" she said. Then her ferocious troop moved behind her as she led them into the dark, dense, and moonlit whispering-woods to an unknown horizon. My eyes chased them as far as they could. My whole body shivered with goose bumps as now I was there stranded forlorn like a defeated gambler.

The retreating howling of the children of darkness somewhere in the deep jungle could still be heard. But their call did not seem as charming and charismatic as Reshma thought. The moon shone clearer now, for the clouds had parted off to let her move freely as she wished, over the forest and the treacherous Krishna River. I stood on the hillock trying to figure out the chain of events. My *Royal Enfield* was still parked under the foot of the hill. *Go home,* sadly said my sad heart.

~

Next evening out of curiosity, I visited the graveyard where Reshma's father was buried. Crossing the thorny hedges, I walked past the other crosses into the direction indicated by her the day we met here—first time. I did not have much trouble, however, in finding the old man's tombstone. But what astonished me more was— another grave on his left. The inscription on it read— *Reshma Goodfellow (1981-2000). Cause of death: Suicide by jumping into the Krishna River. RIP.* The earth seemed to give way beneath my feet as I realized whom I was dating with.

Another flashback incident ran past my mind's eye — how the customers at the other tables were staring at me as we dined at the *Divine Restaurant* a few nights back near Church Gate, while I was talking to Reshma and she was all ears with rapt attention. Were others able to see but me, alone? A chilling sensation ran through my spine and mixed into my blood—now as cold as was Reshma's touch when she'd pushed me into the deathly river.

~

"Nawaz Sahib!" Somebody broke my reverie by calling out my name, as I was parking my Enfield in the courtyard. It was Rajendra, the postman. There was nobody in our entire colony who did not know him. He gave me his usual smile, alighting from his ancient Hero Bicycle. "A letter for you," he said, handing me a sealed yellow envelope. It was from The Third Eye Corporation. I recalled having appeared in an examination for Executive Investigator. I opened the seal and read, it said—I'd cracked the written test and the interview was scheduled next Friday.

"Rajendra Ji," I said, "you've brought good news today, please come in to have a cup of tea." The old man came inside my drawing room to share my happiness. "You'll have to give me a full treat, once you get your final selection," said the silver haired postman, sitting on the couch. But some compartment of my brain was still busy calculating the math of love Reshma had taught me, for her pet wolves and the lethal affection still lingered there. But I thought I still loved her as my mind raced fast—first it said *yes*, then *no* and then a faint *let it go*.

"End"

The Portal Above my Sink

Addison Selna

The face in the mirror is not monstrous
The mouth is not pulled by strings into a snarl
Skin is not broken and bloodied
Eyes don't hold dark secrets of vengeance
The face in the mirror is none of these things
But yet can't be trusted

The mirror leads into a world of lies
A world where that thing lives
Happening to appear at the portal the same time as me
A perfect mimic
Yet in its perfection there is one thing forever locked
away
Never copied

The thoughts locked away in my mind
Are fully mine
This copy could never possibly have a key to the lock
Leave me alone
So another day without glass shattered rooms I'll live
Instead of vengeance contentment is won

Shapeshifting

Stacey-Ann Sukharrie

restlessness
    in my soul,
trembling
    in my toes,
yearning
    in my bones,
itching
    in my skin,
shapeshifting
    conscious,
yet
    slowly drifting, drifting away.

Waiting for the change to happen
    impatience growing,
anticipation blossoming,
    like the seasons turning,
and the moon rising,
    time stays still,
while I become ready,
    to break free,
of the shackles,
    that bind this body.

I hold on to the memory
of this vessel
hoping,
    praying,
        trusting
that I will find my way back
once I'm done exploring.

Faith

Stacey-Ann Sukharrie

I never understood
being taken to church and temple
week after week
being anointed
prayed for, prayed upon, made to pray.

Celebrating all the festivals
from Diwali to Christmas
and everything in between,
enjoying the sweets prepared
with such reverence by those with faith so deep.

I never understood those parents
who advertised their kids' religion
painting them with white chalk on their forehead,
sending them out with crosses and Oms,
forcing them to read the texts,
stories of creation from a time long ago.

I never understood until my child was born.
How can you not believe in God?
When two imperfect people joined
to create a perfect being, breathtaking,
ten fingers, ten toes, a smile so sweet.
Heart breaks to think of it ever wiped away.

I now know why parents anoint their kids
desperately keeping their eyes closed
clasping their hands together
prostrate at the alter
fervently trading promises for their protection.

We try anything and everything
to keep them safe and away from danger.
Fiercely protective like
a pride of lions,
a herd of elephants,
a shepherd with his sheep.

June Full Moon Special

ONE MORE FOR GOOD LUCK

Bryan William Myers

the rabbit chased the sun for spite
spellcheck became a speed bump for fast writers
who can't let go of the past

if you're growing a beard
in the twilight of your own circumspection, leave your
fingers twaddling
along the keys

luck is a set of dice
dangling
from a taxi driver's rearview mirror

on a gray and cloudy day
the coffee gets sucked down into oblivion (which is your
stomach)
as it groans at your second-person personal noun
bullshit

here's a brutal fact: California blondes
never shut the hell up

about a Bandaid they pulled off two weeks ago

and that guy in the corner
saying nothing
knows more than everybody
in town

he stays quiet

I envy him just like the frog in the night searching for flies
there's only so much you can stomach
before you begin to feel
ill

and on that note
always cover your ears
in a foreign town
when an American
drops
by.

En Caul

Dia VanGunten

Like Margaret Mead, I'm fat with memory; hundreds
and hundreds of thousands; millions of memories. I keep
meaning to sit down and actually count them. It would
be strange to bring that upon myself, to let them come at
me willy nilly, good and bad in a great deluge. The 14th
of February: I'm with Mom in the art museum, making
homemade valentines. We press pulp into window
screen and sprinkle flowers. When it dries, rose petals
are embedded into brand new paper. Sometime else,
we're coming home from the lake. Dad's impatient in an
MG convertible. He yells at us to duck so he can drive
beneath a stalled train. Mom says, *"Nope. No fuckin
way."* As she unloads us, the train starts. Dad insists we
would've made it but he's wrong.

Mom gave us life a few times.

Cue Saturday morning cartoons. She-ra and He-man.
Sister and brother. We brandish light spitting swords
and hold them towards the stars. **I HAVE THE
POWER!** The word "power" is a reverberating echo in
the mountains of New Mexico. A rattlesnake catches me
coming outta the outhouse. I close my eyes to the soap.
All the hippies showered at Georgia O'Keeffe's Ghost
Ranch. There's so few ghosts in attendance. I expected
vaginal caves dripping pink-blue-green. I expected
clouds, serene and wobbly like a child's drawing. Op!
Another! The phone rings with congratulations and then
the doorbell. Men exclaim over a giant bottle of
champagne, tall as a toddler, but men can't handle
success. Man of The Hour hulked out. He wrecked the
kitchen and wrestled the stove. He tore O'Keefes Clouds
from the wall. Daytime clouds sailed into the dark yard.

Glass shattered. The stove followed. In the car, I hugged a koala. It was my birthday. I'm newly 9 but I'm back in New Mexico being born. The whole commune is in attendance. Not the guru though, a conspicuous absence. *He's scared of the baby.* Their whispers are giddy with fear. They're already telling a story so I don a costume. I come out in a caul. They claim I made eye contact with everyone in the room except my mother. It was only then that I screamed, as if I recognized them and knew well enough to be afraid. My first assessment of this incarnation was that I was well and truly fucked.

These assholes again?

A caul had currency in that crowd. Folklore calls it a magical signifier. The veiled traveler retains something of her last world and perceives the next. These babies are destined for greatness. They possess darkness. They are bad omens. They are good luck. Is the caul the amulet and the baby the lucky one? Or is the child but a charm? There seems to be some confusion.

This could go on forever. I could never collect everything into one jungian pile. I'm a hoarder in the house of memory. The floorboards bulge with crowded bits. Is it a fire hazard?

My facts: It was my birthday party but I showed up late, after midnight, wearing only a veil. Like Solome. My outfit caused a ruckus. A real hocus pocus. No one noticed the missing afterbirth.

Hard fact: Almost killed my mother. (I grabbed the amniotic sac but left the placenta behind.)

My fictions: A viral tiktok, I'm a puppy with a fluffy voice -- "I was born a dog. I *identify* as a dog. But according to my mom, I'm just a bayyyyby." *bashful batting paw* #itme

Mom texted an article and a fact: *A so-called " Mermaid birth" is rare. Only 1 in 80,000 are born "en caul."* I felt sufficiently special for being born with panache. Mom followed up with three exclamation points. (!!!) In that particular telling of the story, we left out the part where she crawled across the desert. The guru said it was drama. The doctor said it was sepsis.

*

When the Doctors asked about stress, I scoffed. This was a physical thing that was really happening. This was REAL. My actual physical body was malfunctioning. I called them "falling episodes" as if I were a wane Victorian landing on a velvet chaise with a soft plop. I was a balloon sinking to the ground....limp and lilting. It actually felt like that, like I was losing myself in slow motion. I was not especially surprised when this new gravity overtook me.

I'd felt its weight bearing down between my shoulder blades,

*

I got the drifting pauses from Paul who got them from Betty. She'd press her teeth together and lick her lipsticked lips. I feel this in my own face. Mom snaps and says again how she hates it. *Your Dad and Betty did the same thing.* Like them, I'm embarrassed. I'm wounded. I say "I was just thinking" which seems only fair. Mom scowls. She doesn't know what she knows. They're called absences. They're called epilepsy. I never use that word though. I will recall the girl from high school and how the boys used to say **"Throw her in the pool with a box of tide and get yer laundry done."** The first boy to say it was my cruel, clever boyfriend. Obviously I'd prefer to forget that. I thought I was somehow better than her. I didn't know yet that we were both epileptic mopheads who fucked the same guy.

Stigma is the world remembering all the shit, all at once, a great echo of ouch.

I'm blue in Betty's blue kitchen but she's long gone. Uncle Donny's on a jag because I live in a rough neighborhood, where rich white people used to live. Grandpa Floyd and the brothers would rollerskate on the top floor of an old grand. *A ballroom.* Donny mentions which mansion but I have one of my absences. Donny ain't bothered. He launches into a story about Grandpa's Grandpa. The cops were chasing him so he hopped a train. They cornered him in the caboose and he had a fit and fell off the back. Or the cops pushed him and he hit his head on the tracks, had a fit and died. There's always two versions. *We have fits in our family.* I laugh because it's true. One of us is always causing a scene. I ask him about Uncle Herb. Did he marry his aunt or his sister in law? Donny's into genealogy now so he snaps: *I'm your cousin.* I just blink at him.

"Tell Donny how you ignored Floyd's little ticker. He chased after her in his bathrobe screaming 'No granddaughter of mine is gonna drive a death car!' He exposed himself. Robe came undone, colostomy bag and everything."

I explain: "Grandpa said it was a death car because it was a black sports car."

"It was two death cars! One was a head-on collision, the other had a totaled rear end. They soldered two halves together. We got a letter from the state of Michigan."

110

I yawned, a big yowling stretch of the jowls. I yawned

again and again, in painful repetition. Dad said, "Oh I'm

sorry, are we boring you?"

It was a fit: a focal seizure of the frontal lobe. I thought I
was just exhausted, like down to my bones. In my cells,
mitochondria called uncle. *I'm not your uncle, I'm your
cousin. You're not tired, you're dramatic. Drama drama
drama.* This is how you bully the body. Someone taught
my mother and she passed it on to me. Jewelry, quilts,
grandfather clocks, ancestral trauma.

*

I'm back with Betty on beechway. Day of the giant
champagne. Floyd's at the party but Grandma stays with
us. I open presents in Betty's blue kitchen -- a stuffed
koala and magical unicorn stickers. When pressed, the
oily iridescence is misplaced. I blew out 9 candles....no,
wait. It was 8. I had a Holiday Inn slumber party for my
9th birthday. On my 8th birthday, Betty felt sorry for me
so she let us eat sugar cereal. Pink horseshoes floated in
a spoonful of milk. We watched cartoons. A single girl
smurf in a sexist society. Care Bears had it all figured
out: their token characteristic just emblazoned on their
midsections. He-man made his appearance and my
brother leapt to Grandpa's chair. I HAVE THE
POWER! I was too busy with fret and pink horseshoes.
The men were drinking. Betty's dread was contagious.

*

Two men followed me to the gas station and watched
from velveteen seats as I filled Mom's tank. The elder lit
a menthol and diagnosed me as possessed. *She used to*

be so spirited but now she's drained of life force. She's her mother's familiar.

(How dare they? I HAVE THE POWER!!!)

Nah, ya don't. Dad picked you up at the hospital. He took you to inkie's for pizza but you fell out and took the gumball machines down with you. There's gumballs and blood and broken glass. And spilled ink. Inkies. There was a toy capsule and inside, a tiny lantern. Neon green.

Noooo. The lantern was Tucson. You lied to mom because you were too small to be walking to Safeway with pilfered quarters. You're at Dad's now eating the most delicious peach cobbler

from the neighbor's farmstand. Ice cream on top. You'll never know this taste again. You'll put the spoon down when mom calls. *"Where the hell have you been? My car is outta gas!"*

*

When the doctors asked about stress, I laughed. I provided proof of my former vitality. By day, I worked at an inner city day camp. By night, I was a cocktail waitress at a jazz club. I was a workout addict, a daughter, a sister. I was the proprietor of Velvet Elvis, the city's only vintage clothing store. Through it all, I was a 4.0 honors student. (Mom and I were a power duo on campus. We attended the same classes. I was an academic wingman.) I didn't do everything all at once but it feels that way. I packed it in because I didn't have long to be that person.

Doc scribbled as my sisters slipped past the curtains.

They curled goose-prickled shoulders. "Mom won't

come in. She says you're faking. She says to say she

knows." They hung their heads. The doctor made another notation.

"You're not allowed to be sick. Mom's already the sick one."

They knew the drill. We were supposed to feel her pain over our own. She hijacked our nervous systems. She keened all night while we begged her to stay on Earth. She had nothing to live for. We struck life and death bargains that expired every 24hrs. It was a grim quotidian task. The doctor surveyed my sisters, their terror and disarray. They needed haircuts. I reached for my gaggle but the doctor said, *"Girls, go get your mother."* She'd already driven off in a huff, squealing wheels and burning rubber.

I jumped to my own defense: "It's not psychosomatic. It's physical. It's *in* my body."

I sound like the killer in the 80's movie about the babysitter. *The caller is inside the house.* The doctor said, *"Stress isn't helping."* I didn't like his knowing look. I'd just met him but he'd already seen too much. I called my sisters close and tugged my gown past the two patches with metal nubs. *"Don't mind my new bionic nipples."* They laughed and leaned against the bed.

The doctor said, "Something's gotta give."

I packed it in because....*rebellion.* I planted flags on the mantle of identity.

Proof of life had overtaxed the machine. Mom was wrong. It wasn't an invention. I wasn't looking for attention. I wanted release. I still wonder if it's just a ruse to get rest. I even asked a neurologist if maybe I might've faked the EEG results by "trancing out" during the two hour test. *No kiddo, that's not how it works.* He tells me my brain spikes 6 times every so many seconds.

*

I once slipped into momentary despair because I was stupefied by mittens, what they were or why I had them. Gloves would've been an easy guess. Long term memory was locked away safe but short term memory was a sieve. I stopped reading fiction. Couldn't follow the story. I abandoned a novel. Couldn't tell the story. I stopped ordering pizza because I once forgot my address. I moved out of my beloved 4th floor walk-up. I wasn't dying on those stairs. I didn't answer 3am calls because I couldn't drive. No more groggy runs to the gas station. Eventually the seizures waned. Short term memory returned and long term memory unlocked.

I got a motorcycle and started writing fiction again.

*

Inside a toy capsule, a tiny lantern glimmers neon green. I try to hide it from my mother.

The radio says there's a kodachrome -- a rainbow! -- but mama is gonna take it away. The holographic universe says it can never forget itself because there's a galaxy in every star. Ego insists there's a primordial essence that sets each person apart. If you're old enough to see yourself in babies then you know the smallest portion holds the whole. Each shard of self is a gestalt record. A gob of slime carries the genome. Identical twins meet in Minnesota for the first time. Their similarities prove that "personhood" is DNA. At best, we're a random jumble of genetic components that makes us different from our sisters.

Self is essentially unstable. There is no fixed point of being. Time isn't linear and "personality" is a process. Identity is a turning wheel, a tilting windmill. It's dutch tulips and portuguese fishes. *As far as I know.* The Greeks think I'm Greek. I tell them I'm from the Azores and they clap their hands. That settles that. The semen of seamen! I don't spit into a tube because I want that clap to be true -- a lie in the sunshine. Coming off the train in Piraeus, we smelled strawberries. It's been years since a strawberry smelled like itself. We buy them and shiver. The sun is setting and a winter wind is whipping off the water. Greece is cold in December.

Fire is feasting on New Mexico. A controlled burn got out of control and joined forces with a flame that laid dormant underground before rising up in fury. She burned slow through three snows, three melts. Under the wildflowers, down deep, she was a red hot ember. That whole time, she was sparking. A seizure. A tendon turns in my right eye, like a jump rope, and hurts for days after. Gumballs are rolling. Clouds are flying. Who am I?

I thought I knew that much at least but what a naive notion. We're warped by the lies we tell to protect the people we love.

Life is bundled memories. Brain is the turtle that holds up the whole world. How many selves have I been already, just in this one single life? My story is 1000 stories. These stories can be told thousands of ways. Heroes and villains are trading cards, easily swapped.

115

Authors

MEHREEN AHMED is an Australian novelist born in Bangladesh. Her historical fiction, The Pacifist, is a Drunken Druid's Editor's Choice and an Amazon Audible bestseller. Gatherings is nominated for the James Tait Black Prize for fiction. Her short and flash fiction have won in The Waterloo Festival Competition, Cabinet-of-Heed Stream-Of-Consciousness Challenge, shortlisted, finalist, nominated for the 3xbotN, Pushcart, Publication of the Month, Honorable Mentions. Also, critically acclaimed by Midwest Book Review, DD Magazine, The Wild Atlantic Book Club to name a few. She is a juror to the KM Anthru International Prize.

Page 20

PAULINE AKSAY is a storyteller based in Toronto, Canada. She has experience in writing poetry, digital animation, and in illustrating children's books, and has previously received two artist's grants to write, illustrate and self-publish two children's stories. Aksay's work explores mental health, perception, imagination, and the limits of memory, offering an evocative glimpse into the human experience from the eyes of an outsider. She aspires to promote the emotional intelligence, compassion, and understanding in the people who experience her work.

Page 6

RAMMEL CHAN is an actor and writer based in Chicago. He is a Kundiman Fiction Fellow and his short plays have premiered at the Gift Theater as part of TEN and his fiction has appeared in Asimov's Science Fiction, Riksha and is forthcoming in the Tiger Moth Review. He has performed with the Timeline Theater, Lookingglass Theater Company, the Goodman Theater, Victory Gardens Theater and with the Steppenwolf Theater Company, among others. He also recently co-starred in the film I Used To Go Here. Please say hi at rammelchan.com

Page 8

WILLIAM E. HESTION is a poet, sketch artist, and up-and-coming filmmaker from Philadelphia, PA.

Much of his work is based in finding spiritual influence in everyday life.

Page 15; Page 17; Page 76

HASIB IFTEKHAR is a writer currently based in North York, Toronto. Working towards his debut novel, his previous publishing credits are with Canadian literary magazine and anthology collections. He loves to spend time with his family, read, and gauge around for values and sentiments, or a lack thereof.

Page 62

DANI KEI JOCHUMS is a Hapa writer, nonprofit worker, and all-around dabbler residing in Portland, Oregon. Her fiction and academic writing delves into the nuances of identity, perspective, and dependence. When she's not writing, she can be found making new connections in the community or kicking it with her two cats.

Page 29

ZIAUL MOID KHAN is a speculative fiction author and a romantic poet from the North India countryside, Johri. He considers himself a world citizen. His work has been featured in Bards and Sages Quarterly, Literary Orphans, Better Than Starbucks, To Live Again: An Anthology, and other venues. Zia teaches English Literature, residing in Jaipur, Rajasthan with his beautiful wife, Khushboo Khan and a five-years-young & cute son, Brahamand Cosmos. He does not drink, nor does he smoke but his characters do all sorts of things including but not limited to intoxication. Email him at ziamoidkhan.b@gmail.com.

Page 88

LAUREN KLEIN is a writer and illustrator from Tkaronto. Her poetry and fiction have appeared or will soon appear in Forage, CommuterLit, Flash Fiction Magazine, and more. She is currently writing a novel. Find her online at @fruit_stains.

Page 64

MARINA LOPEZ is a Pittsburgh-based Mexican composer, educator, and budding writer. She is interested in challenging borders between musical genres and between art forms, to create immersive experiences that challenge the listeners' preconceptions. She is currently working with Volta Music Foundation, which seeks to make music education accessible to students in need in Latin America and create music programs that help underserved communities in the U.S.

Page 69; Page 71; Page 74

MAKENZIE MACROL is in college, but she lives each day not only as a student of her institution, but as a student of the world. She is, most recently, the author of the poem "red," which was published in Solstice Literary Magazine's debut issue and achieved first place in the magazine's spring poetry contest of 2022. Macrol is no stranger to difficult subjects; by exploring love, life, and cultural issues, her goal is to spark new and necessary conversation around what makes people struggle—what makes people human.

Page 78; Page 79; Page 80

BRYAN WILLIAM MYERS traveled to 12 countries in 2019. He spent most of the pandemic in Vietnam, writing poems, stories, plays, his first full-length screenplay, and a pilot he optioned to an app startup for $500. He's self-published 15 books. His first chapbook of poems, Empty Beer Cans: Quarantine Poems from Da Nang, Vietnam, will be released in May 2022 by Alien Buddha Press.

Page 102

RIS V. ROSE is a 23-year-old poet, fiction writer, and editor. She is a Writer in Residence for Culturally Arts and has had 8 poems published with The Soap Box Press. Her first collection of poetry, Supernova, is about how a special kind of love can spread like sunlight into all the craters in our lives, just to lead to the destructive kind of heartbreak that rips apart our entire world, like a black hole.

Page 81; Page 83; Page 84

ADDISON SELNA is an emerging author. As he nears his first year of college Addison is preparing for a life filled with art, literature, and the laughter of strangers. He has recently focused his creative attention on the image of mirrors and the easy deception they create. He looks as well to the counterculture movement of the 60s for inspiration. Find him online @addisonselna.

Page 98

STACEY-ANN SUKHARRIE was born and raised in the Twin Islands of Trinidad & Tobago, Stacey-Ann Sukharrie migrated to Canada as a pre-teen. Her writing is informed by personal experiences, ongoing connection to both birth and adoptive countries and educational background (Honors Bachelor of Arts from the University of Toronto- Major in English Literature/Double Minor in Women's Studies and

119

Political Sciences). She has been employed in the Financial Services Industry for the last 20 years. Stacey-Ann is passionate about empowering humans and leads authentically in all aspects of her life. She enjoys giving back to the community via volunteer work with a focus on diversity initiatives.

Page 99; Page 100

DIA VANGUNTEN did not eat pink horseshoes on her 8th birthday. She does write magical realism. "En Caul" is part of a larger project that explores the stories we tell, the stories we don't tell and how we mythologize to survive.

Page 104

Lightning Source UK Ltd.
Milton Keynes UK
UKHW020734270622
405010UK00002B/4

9 781957 960029